AF221096

NOTHING

THE GIFT YOU
TRULY
WISHED FOR

FSC
www.fsc.org
MIX
Papier aus ver-
antwortungsvollen
Quellen
Paper from
responsible sources
FSC® C105338

Originally published in Germany as *Nichts: Das Geschenk, das Du Dir gewünscht hast* by Caroline Stern, BoD – Books on Demand, Norderstedt, in 2018.
Copyright © 2018 by Caroline Stern.
Reprint: 2020.
Cover, translation and design by Caroline Stern, Berlin, Germany.
Printed and published by: BoD – Books on Demand, Norderstedt.
www.bod.de
ISBN: 978-3-752-80460-7.